W9-CQA-994

Holt

ELEMENTARY SCIENCE

Joseph Abruscato   Joan Wade Fossaceca
Jack Hassard   Donald Peck

HOLT, RINEHART AND WINSTON, PUBLISHERS
New York • Toronto • London • Sydney

THE AUTHORS

Joseph Abruscato
Associate Dean
College of Education and Social Services
University of Vermont
Burlington, Vermont

Joan Wade Fossaceca
Teacher
Pointview Elementary School
Westerville City Schools
Westerville, Ohio

Jack Hassard
Professor
College of Education
Georgia State University
Atlanta, Georgia

Donald Peck
Supervisor of Science
Woodbridge Township School District
Woodbridge, New Jersey

Editorial Development William N. Moore, Lois Eskin, Roger R. Rogalin, Stephanie S. Blank
Editorial Processing Margaret M. Byrne, Regina Chilcoat, Shelley L. Feiler, Dorrie K. Berkowitz
Art and Production Vivian Fenster, Fred C. Pusterla, Robin Swenson, Susan Gombocz
Product Managers Ronald E. Suchodolski, John W. M. Cooke
Advisory Board John Boynton, Max Callahan, Glenn Hartman, Norman Hughes, Albert LeFevre, Douglas Nash, Jon Permar, Dennis Spurgeon
Consultant John Matejowsky
Researchers Pamela Floch, Gerard LaVan

Photo and art acknowledgments appear on page 136.
Cover photograph by Stouffer Productions/Animals, Animals.

THE CONSULTANTS

Content Consultants

Edward E. C. Clebsch, Ph.D.
Professor of Botany
University of Tennessee
Knoxville, Tennessee

Jerry Faughn, Ph.D.
Professor of Physics
Eastern Kentucky University
Richmond, Kentucky

Ellen M. Herron, Ph.D.
Assistant Director
Lamont-Doherty Geological Observatory
Palisades, New York

Margaret A. LeMone, Ph.D.
Scientist
National Center for Atmospheric Research
Boulder, Colorado

W. T. Lippincott, Ph.D.
Professor of Chemistry
University of Arizona
Tucson, Arizona

Gary Peterson, D.A.
Assoc. Professor of Biology
South Dakota State University
Brookings, South Dakota

Arne E. Slettebak
Professor of Astronomy
Ohio State University
Columbus, Ohio

Gordon Taylor
Principal
Estey School
Saskatoon, Saskatchewan

Teacher Consultants

Peggy Ann Archacki
Assistant Supervisor of Science
Cleveland Public Schools
Cleveland, Ohio

Thomas L. Beck
Teacher
Evening Street Elementary School
Worthington, Ohio

Lynn T. Cluff
Teacher
Central School
South Burlington, Vermont

Linda Coffey, Ph.D.
Director of Early Childhood Ed.
Broward County Public Schools
Broward County, Florida

Marcia Lambek
Teacher
School One
Scotch Plains, New Jersey

Carole Rutland
Teacher
Muscogee County Public Schools
Columbus, Georgia

Judy Woodward
Science Advisor
Delevan Science Center
Los Angeles City Schools
Los Angeles, California

Rina Zucker
Teacher
Ashford Elementary School
Houston, Texas

Reading Consultants

Paul Greenfield
Associate Professor
English and Humanities
Dutchess Community College
Poughkeepsie, New York

Judith Linscott Martin
Reading Specialist
Montgomery County Public Schools
Montgomery County, Maryland

Evelyn Mason
Elementary Language Arts Supervisor
Indianapolis Public Schools
Indianapolis, Indiana

PILOT SCHOOLS

We gratefully acknowledge the help of the teachers and students who field-tested portions of the Holt Elementary Science program in the spring of 1977. Their comments and criticisms were used to improve the program. The field teachers were:

Margaret Rodriquez
Encinal School
Morgan Hill, CA

Viola Sando
Murphy School
Stamford, CT

Lenore Ambrose
Palmetto El Sch
Miami, FL

Judy Kaplan
Lake Stevens El Sch
OpaLock, FL

Beth Williams
Laura Childs El Sch
Bloomington, IN

David Allen
Howard C. Reiche Sch
Portland, ME

Stephanie Barnhart
Immac Heart of Mary Sch
Towson, MD

John Cooney
Mill Swan El Sch
Worcester, MA

Eileen Martin
Stearns School
Pittsfield, MA

Phil Maines
Fountain El Sch
Grand Rapids, MI

Olivia McKinney
Vernor El Sch
Detroit, MI

Ellen Stob
Hillcrest El Sch
Grand Rapids, MI

Dennis Davis
Portland El Sch
Richfield, MN

Gary Hawkins
Cambridge El Sch
Cambridge, MN

M. Foster
Green Trails Sch
Chesterfield, MO

A. J. Sullivan
Ferguson Florissant Sch Dist
Ferguson, MO

Rick Ashworth
Choteau School
Choteau, MT

Nancy Ritter
Fort Benton Sch
Ft. Benton, MT

J. Ely
Burgess School
Berlin, NH

Edward Douglas
Sumner El Sch
Camden, NJ

Nancy Hearst
Pennypacher El Sch
Willingboro, NJ

Lee Ferrera
St. Jerome Sch
Brooklyn, NY

Robert Kase
Public School 178
Jamaica, NY

Lois Parker
Bloomfield El Sch
Holcomb, NY

Lorraine Sharp
95th Street School
Niagara Falls, NY

Paul Snyder
93rd Street School
Niagara Falls, NY

Helen Suchy
Theo Roosevelt El Sch
Binghamton, NY

Edward Wianecki
School 43
Buffalo, NY

Patricia Brazas
Peck El Sch
Greensboro, NC

Ann Schwabeland
Irving Park El Sch
Greensboro, NC

Bernice Perry
Brooks El Sch
Raleigh, NC

John Foley
Lewis and Clark Sch
Fargo, ND

Manna Hay
Arlington Sch
Toledo, OH

Charles Knepshield
Taft El Sch
Middletown, OH

Dawn Rowe
Brush El Sch
Grafton, OH

Ross Neidich
West Branch El Sch
Bradford, PA

Frank Rice, Jr.
Westview El Sch
Spartanburg, SC

Wilma Todd
Cooper El Sch
Garland, TX

James Goodwin
East Salem Sch
Salem, VA

Dean Rickabaugh
Highland Park Sch
Roanoke, VA

Patricia Kinner
St. Aemilian's Sch
Milwaukee, WI

Kathryn Lee
Falk El Sch
Madison, WI

Many thanks also to the principals, supervisors, and science coordinators who assisted in the arrangements for the field test.

CONTENTS

SEE AND TOUCH

① COLOR

Color helps you group things.

Color tells you when to walk.
Color tells you when to wait.

Color can tell you
what to eat.

What else can
color tell you?

1. Find colored things.

2. Put each thing in the right bag.

② SHAPE

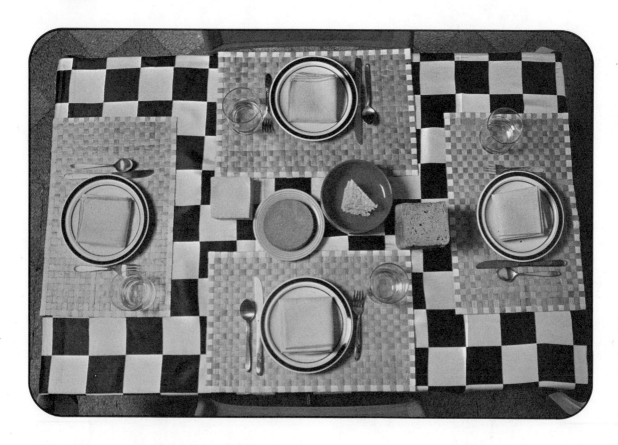

All things have **shape**.
Find these shapes.

Shapes tell us things.

The arrow tells you which way you can go.

What do the other signs tell you?

1. Walk around the room.

2. Find these shapes.

3. Put the shapes in the right box.

③ SIZE

Some things are **big**.

Some are **small**.

What **sizes** do you see?

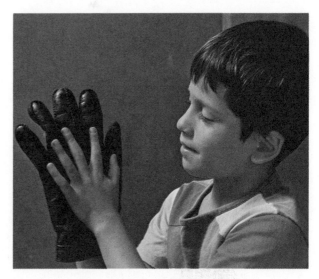

You can tell size by looking.

You can **measure** size.

How does size
help the man?

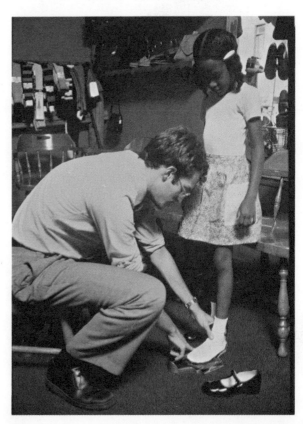

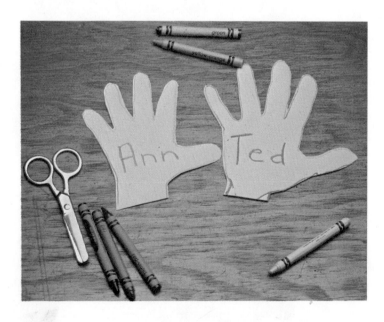

1. Trace your hand.

2. Cut it out.

3. Look at your friend's hand.

4. Whose hand is bigger?

5. Whose hand is smaller?

④ TOUCH

The rabbit is **soft**.

The rock is **hard**.

How do other things feel?

Which chair would you like to sit in?   Why?

We use **rough** things.
We use **smooth** things.
You can **group** things by
the way they feel.

1. Take something out of the bag.

2. Feel it.

3. Put it near the right card.

⑤ WEIGHT

The couch is **heavy**.

The chair is **light**.

How do you know?

The lady is heavier.

How do you know?

These people **weigh** things.

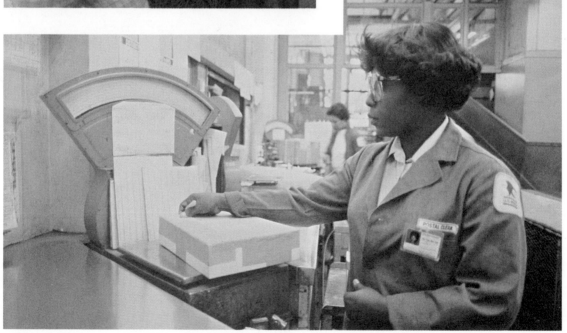

Weighing tells you how heavy things are.

⑥ SORTING

What do you see?

How do things look and feel?

We can **sort** things by the way they look
and feel.

Tell how these things are sorted.

MAIN IDEAS

- ○ We learn by looking.

- ○ We learn by touching.

- ○ We learn by measuring.

- ○ We can sort things by the way they look.

- ○ We can sort things by the way they feel.

QUESTIONS

1. Name two things we sort by color.

2. Name four shapes. Find them in picture 4 .

3. What is bigger than you? What is smaller?

4. How can you tell how big a thing is?

5. What is rough, smooth, soft, and hard in picture 5?

6. How can you tell how heavy a thing is?

7. Name five ways to sort things.

SOMETHING EXTRA

Some people are blind.
They read by touch.
Their books have no words.
The pages have dots.
The dots stick up.
Blind people feel the dots.
The dots spell words.

UNIT 2

TIME AND PLACE

①YESTERDAY, TODAY, AND TOMORROW

This happened **yesterday**.

This is happening **today**.

This will happen **tomorrow**.

Yesterday.

Today.

Yesterday is gone.
Today is right now.
Tomorrow comes after
today.

Tomorrow.

25

1. What happened yesterday?

2. What is happening today?

3. What will happen tomorrow?

4. Put these pictures in order.

② DAYTIME, NIGHTTIME

In the **daytime** it is light.

In the **nighttime** it is dark. Sometimes you see the moon and the stars.

One **day** has a daytime and a nighttime.

Nighttime changes to daytime.

Daytime changes to nighttime.

1. What do you do in the daytime?

2. What do you do in the nighttime?

3. Draw a picture and color it.

③ TIME

A **clock** tells us the **time** of day.

What time do you come to school?

What time do you eat lunch?

What time do you go to sleep?

We do different things at different times of the day.

1. Put your head on your desk.

2. Raise your hand when you think a minute has gone by.

4 A WEEK, A MONTH, A YEAR

OCTOBER

Sunday	Monday	Tuesday	Wednesday	Thursday	Friday	Saturday
1	2	3	4	5	6	7
8	9	10	11	12	13 Baseball Game	14
15	16	17 JOHN'S Birthday	18	19	20	21
22	23	24	25	26	27	28
29	30	31				

A **week** is made of seven days.
Can you name the days?

This is one **month**.
How many weeks are there?

There are twelve months in one **year**.
Can you name the months?

There are four **seasons** in a year.
Can you name them?

⑤ WHERE IS IT?

The girls are in **front** of the fence.
The house is in **back** of the fence.

The boy is climbing **over** the fence.
The grass is **under** the fence.

1. Look at the picture.

2. What is under the bridge?

3. What is over the bridge?

4. What is in front of the blue boat?

5. What is in back of the blue boat?

⑥ NEAR AND FAR

The seesaw is **far**.
The swings are **near**.
How do you know?

Far things look small.
Near things look big.

What is near?
What is far?

MAIN IDEAS

○ Yesterday has passed. Today is now. Tomorrow will come.

○ One day has a daytime and a nighttime.

○ We can tell time in weeks, months, and years.

○ The words front, back, over, and under tell where things are.

○ The words far and near tell where things are.

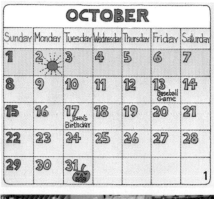

QUESTIONS

1. What day comes before today? What day comes after today?

2. What does it look like outside in the daytime?

3. What things can you sometimes see in the sky at night?

4. What do we use to help us tell time?

5. Name the days of the week.

6. Name the four seasons of the year.

7. Look at picture 4 . Tell what things are over, under, near, and far.

SOMETHING EXTRA

There are many kinds of clocks.

Sometimes they break.

Some people fix and sell clocks.

This man has a clock store.

He is fixing a clock.

UNIT
3
WHERE WE LIVE

① MOUNTAINS, FORESTS, VALLEYS

Mountains are high places.

Forests can grow on mountains.

Forests have trees.

A **valley** is a place between mountains. A valley can have a river in it.

It gets colder as you go up a mountain.
It is cool in a forest.
The trees give shade.

eagle

owl

bear

mountain goat

mountain lion

deer

rabbit

chipmunk

Many animals live in forests,
mountains, and valleys.

What animals do you see?

② THE PLAINS

The **plains** are very **flat**.
The plains have few trees.

In the summer the plains are dry and hot.

In the winter the plains are cold.

Grass grows on the plains.

Some animals eat the grass for food.

coyote

buffalo

snake

prairie dog

mouse

ground squirrel

These animals live on the plains.
Can you name them?

③ THE DESERT

A **desert** is hot and dry.
Very little rain falls.
The plants and animals need very
little water.

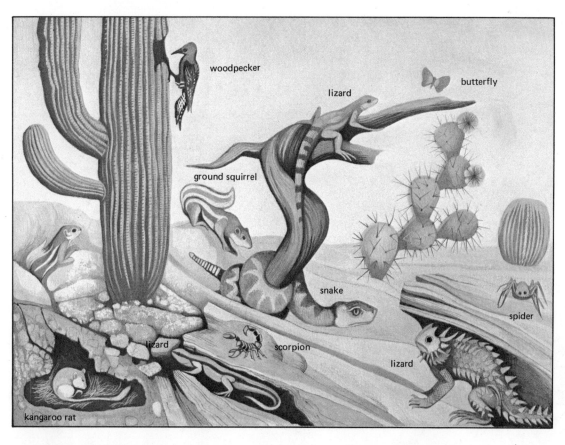

woodpecker

butterfly

lizard

ground squirrel

snake

spider

lizard

scorpion

lizard

kangaroo rat

Many animals live in the desert.
Some live in the ground.
What desert animals can you
name?

This is a **cactus** plant.
It lives in the desert.
Many desert plants
keep water inside.

1. Look inside a cactus.

2. See what is there.

④ AT THE SEA

At the **sea**
it can be rocky.

At the sea it can be sandy.

The wind blows
at the sea.

In summer people go to the sea.
It is cool there.

Plants grow at the sea.
This plant is called **seaweed**.

These animals live at the sea.
They live on the sand and in the water.
Can you name them?

⑤ PEOPLE, PLACES, AND THINGS

A farmer is growing food in the valley.

These people are catching fish in the sea.

This cowboy works on the plains.

People work in different places.

These men are cutting trees.

This woman makes pretty things.

This woman is building a boat.

1. Look at the pictures.

2. Where do these people work?

⑥ HAVING FUN

These people are having fun.

What are these people doing?

Where are they having fun?

People can have fun in many places.
Where do you have fun?

1. Make a fun chart.

2. Find pictures of people having fun outside.

3. Put the pictures in the right place.

MAIN IDEAS

○ There are many different places on our earth.

○ Each place has its own kind of weather.

○ Each place has certain animals and plants living there.

○ In each place people may work and play differently.

QUESTIONS

1. Which place is higher, a mountain or a valley?

2. Where is it warmer on a mountain?
Where is it colder?

3. Name a plant that grows on the plains.

4. What is the weather like in the desert?

5. Why does a cactus keep water inside it?

6. Name two animals that live at the sea.

7. Look at picture 5. Where do these
people work?

SOMETHING EXTRA

This is a very cold place.

Ice and snow are on the ground all the time.

It is called the Arctic.

Polar bears live there.

They have thick fur coats that keep them warm.

UNIT 4

AIR AND WATER

① AIR

Air is all around us.
We need air to live.

There is air in this glass.

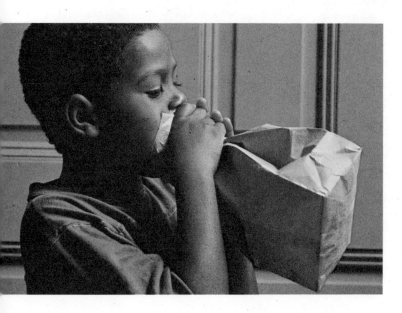

There is air in
this bag.

Can you see air?
How do you know it is there?

We can weigh air.
Which balloon has more air?
Which balloon weighs more?

1. Put paper in a cup.

2. Turn the cup upside down.

3. Put it in some water.

4. Take the cup out of the water.

5. Feel the paper towel.
   Is it wet or dry?

② USING AIR

Air can help us.

Air can hurt us.

Moving air is called **wind**.
Wind can move things.

We use air in many ways.
How can we use air?

1. Make a fan.

2. Use the fan to make wind.

3. What can you move with your fan?

③ WATER

Water is all around us.

We need water to live.

Where do you see water?

Water can look like this.

Water can look like this.

Water can look like this.

76

The water is tall like the glass.

The water
is flat like
the pan.

Water does not have its own shape.

1. Make ice cubes that are good to eat.

2. Leave one in a dish.

3. See what happens.

④ USING WATER

Water can help us.

Water can hurt us.

We use water to **travel**.

We use water
for fun.

We use water in many ways.
In what ways do we use water?

⑤ AIR, WATER, PLANTS, AND ANIMALS

All plants and animals need air to live.

All plants and animals need water to live.

These plants and animals live in water.

The **seeds** of this plant are carried by air.

1. Grow a plant with air and water.

2. Grow a plant without air and water.

3. See what happens.

⑥ CLEANING UP

In some places our air and water are
dirty.

Dirty air and water are bad for people, plants, and animals.

How can we help clean up our air and
water?

MAIN IDEAS

- ◯ Air and water are all around us.

- ◯ All living things need air and water.

- ◯ People use air and water in many ways.

- ◯ People can keep our air and water clean.

QUESTIONS

1. What do we call moving air?

2. How do we know the wind is blowing?

3. Name three ways we use air.

4. Name three ways we use water.

5. How do plants and animals use air and water?

6. Why should we keep our air and water clean?

7. How can we help keep our air and water clean?

SOMETHING EXTRA

Most airplanes land on the ground.

This airplane is special.

It flies in the air.

It lands on the water.

LOOKING AT YOU

① HOW DO WE LOOK?

People look **alike** in many ways.
How do these boys look alike?

Jack and Jill are friends.
How are they alike?
How are they **different**?

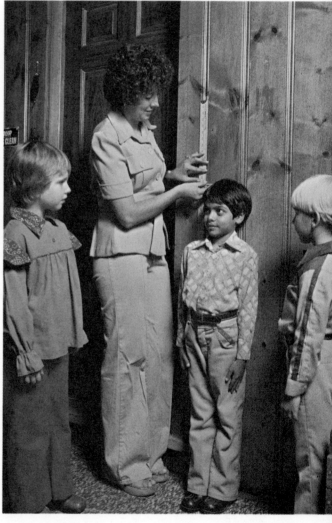

People are different in many ways.
How are these people different?

There is only one you.
You are special.

1. How are you special?

2. Make a fingerprint and see.

② GROWING AND CHANGING

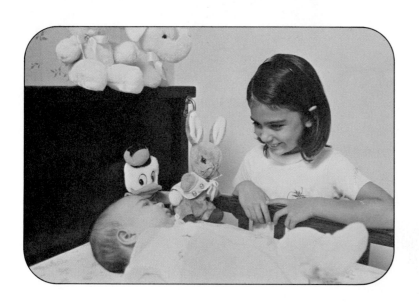

You are growing.
You **change** as you
grow.

Some people grow faster than others.

How have you grown?
How have you changed?

1. Have a friend trace your shape on paper.

2. Cut out the shape.

3. Color the shape.

4. How is your shape like your friend's shape?

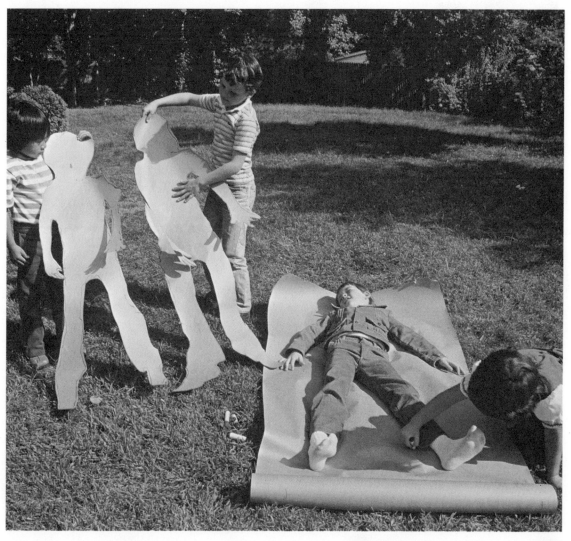

③ EATING GOOD FOODS

Foods help us grow.
Foods are fun to eat.

Foods come from plants.

Foods come from animals.

1. Find pictures of foods that are good for you.

2. Plan a meal.

④ STAYING HEALTHY

Running, jumping, and playing ball can be good for you.

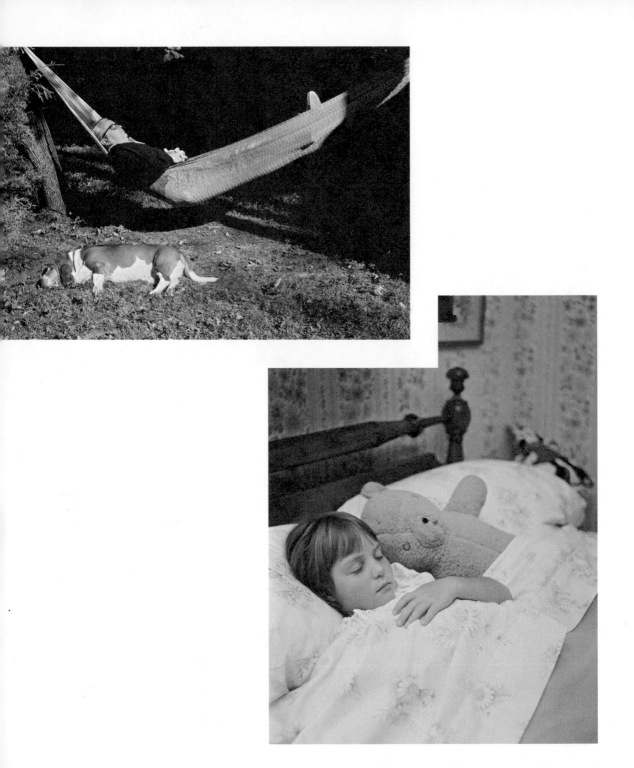

Everyone needs **rest** from work and play.

Staying **clean** keeps us **healthy.**

5 A PLACE TO LIVE

We all need a place to live.

We need a place to eat.

We need a place to sleep.

We need a place that is warm
and dry.

People live in many kinds of houses.
Houses can be made of many
different things.

⑥ WHAT DO YOU LIKE?

Some people like the same things.
Some people like different things.

These two boys are friends.
Sometimes they like the same things.
Sometimes they like different things.
Do you like all the same things as
your friends?

ACTIVITY

ur favorite things to do in school
Like
Dont Like
Math
2
2
2. Reading
3
1
3. Spelling
1
3
ience
2
2
MODERN PHYSICS
HUMAN PHYSIOLOGY
HRW

1. What do you like?

2. What don't you like?

MAIN IDEAS

○ We are alike and different in many ways.

○ We change as we grow.

○ We all need food and a place to live.

○ We need to rest and keep clean to stay healthy.

○ We all do not like the same things.

QUESTIONS

1. Name three ways people are alike.

2. Name three ways people are different.

3. How do people change as they grow?

4. What are the four food groups?

5. Name a food that belongs in each group.

6. What do we need to stay healthy?

7. Do we all have to like the same things?

SOMETHING EXTRA

This woman is a baby doctor.

She helps babies stay healthy.

She helps babies when they are sick.

Like all of us, babies need good food, rest, and love to stay healthy.

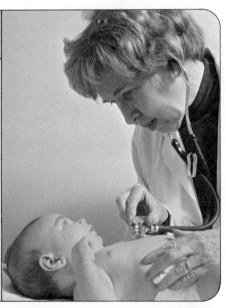

6

LOOKING AT PLANTS AND ANIMALS

①LIVING . . . NOT LIVING

Plants are living things.

Animals are living things.

Living things move and need air.

Living things need food.

Living things grow.

These things are not living.
How do you know?

Which things are living?
Which things are not living?

1. Find pictures of living things.

2. Find pictures of things that are not living.

3. Put them on the right chart.

② HOW ANIMALS LOOK DIFFERENT

Animals look different in many ways.

They are different colors.

They are big.

They are small.

This animal has soft **fur**.

This animal has a hard
shell.

How does this animal
look to you?

118

The rabbit is the same color as the snow.

The rabbit is hard to see.

How does this keep the rabbit safe?

What helps this animal stay safe?

③ WHERE ANIMALS LIVE

Animals live in many places.

Some live in **trees**.

Some live in the **ground**.

Some live in water.

Some animals live in more than one
place.
A frog lives in water and on land.

Where do these animals live?

Make a home for an animal.

4 HOW ANIMALS MOVE

Animals move
in many ways.

A rabbit **hops**.

A fish **swims**.

Some animals move fast.   Some animals move slowly.

Some animals move in more than one way.

A duck can swim, fly, and walk.

124

1. Look at the picture.

2. How do these animals move?

3. Try to move like them.

⑤ PLANTS

Plants are all around us.
Some are small.
Some are big.

Plants have many shapes.
Plants have many colors.

This plant has a
rough stem.

This plant has a
smooth stem.

How do other plants feel to you?

128

⑥ MORE ABOUT PLANTS

This tree has big leaves.

This tree has **needle** leaves.

This plant has red **flowers**.

This plant has orange **fruit**.

Many plants grow from **seeds**.

Can you see the seeds on this plant?

1. Draw your own plant.

2. Use parts of plants in your picture.

MAIN IDEAS

○ Plants and animals are living things.

○ Animals are different in many ways.

○ Animals live in many places.

○ Animals move in different ways.

○ Plants are different in many ways.

○ Some plants have leaves, flowers, fruits, and seeds.

1. What things are living?

2. Name a big animal and a small animal.

3. How does a rabbit keep itself safe?

4. How is a turtle different from a cat?

5. How does a duck move? How do other animals move?

6. How are plants different from each other?

7. Name three parts of a plant.

SOMETHING EXTRA

This farmer has many sheep.

He is giving this sheep a haircut.

The man will save the wool from the sheep.

People use the wool to make clothes.

4 crayons = 38.6 grams

THINK METRIC

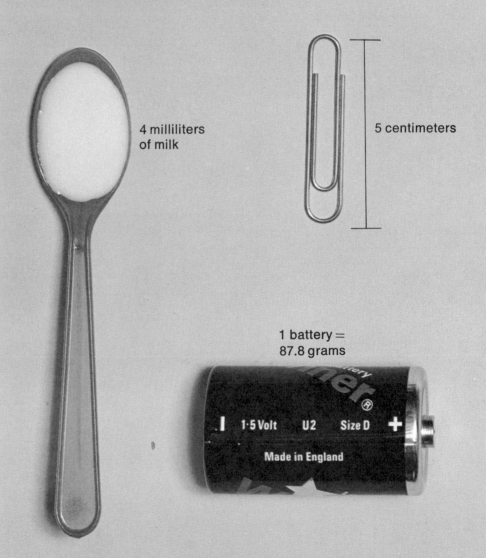

4 milliliters
of milk

5 centimeters

1 battery =
87.8 grams

1·5 Volt U2 Size D +

Made in England

3 jacks = 5.5 grams

PASTEURIZED
HOMOGENIZED
VITAMIN D
MILK

PASTEURIZED
HOMOGENIZED
VITAMIN D
MILK

HALF PINT (236 ml)

4 of these = about 1 liter

13.75 centimeters

PHOTO CREDITS

ART CREDITS